Dear friend,

Our designers put a lot of time and effort into creating each outfit, so that it is trendy, easy to cut-out, and fun to play with.

We wish this book will help you express your unique personality through fashion.

Please feel free to leave a review on Amazon. Add photos if you'd like. We can't wait to see the styles you created!!

Thank you!

Visit our website for FREE colouring
step-by-step tutorials and printables:
lucky-designs.com/links
or scan the QR code:

Acknowledgements: macrovector & brgfx / Freepik

Enjoy hours of fun dressing the paper doll models in different outfits, thanks to this fanciest colouring book.

How to use this book:

Step 1

Cut out the dolls from the back cover.
On the last pages of this book, you will find two stand templates.
Follow the instructions to attach the stands to your dolls.

Step 2

Pull out the pages inside this book and color the clothes using your favorite art supplies.

Step 3

Cut out the outfits. Dress the dolls and start playing!

FANCY!

AMAZING

You are super

TALENTED

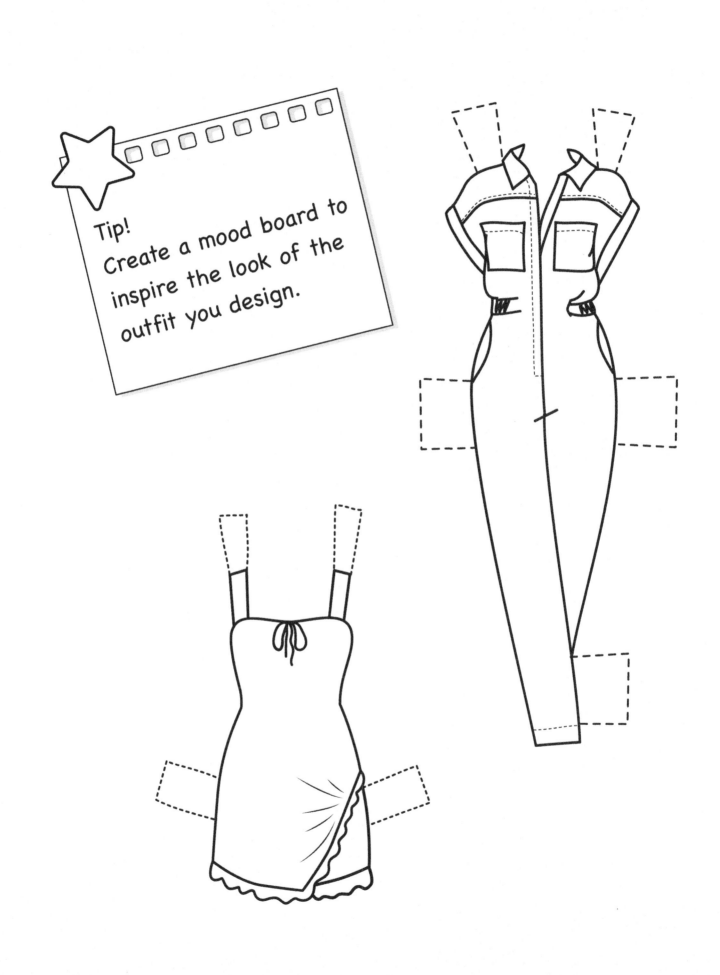

Tip!
Create a mood board to inspire the look of the outfit you design.

WOW!

LOOKS GOOD!

Make a fashion statement!

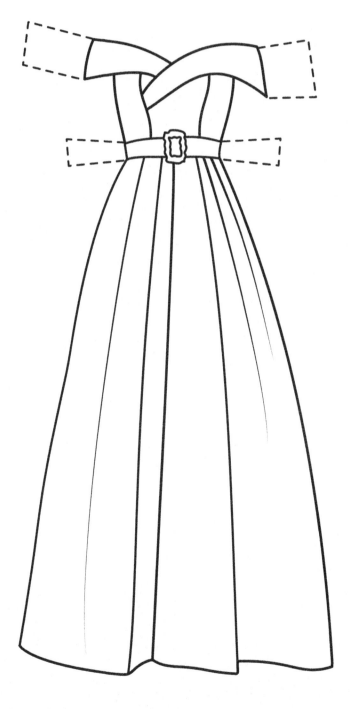

Athleisure Fashion Style

The Athleisure style combines the words "athletic" and "leisure". It combines activewear with everyday clothes.

This style is characterized by simple but elegant designs that show versatility and a dynamic lifestyle.

It became widespread in 2016 when key influencers Beyoncé and Rihanna introduced it to the mainstream.

Turning performance wear into everyday wear, athleisure is blurring the lines between the clothes you'd wear to the gym and those you'd wear to lunch.

Don't be afraid to experiment with colour combinations. Let your imagination run wild...

Feminine Fashion Style

The feminine fashion style is the ultimate celebration of everything girly.

The feminine woman is ladylike, delicate, and youthful with the image of innocence and compassion.

The feminine style consists mostly of skirts and dresses, predominant pastel tones and embraces cute details, softness, drape, and curls.

Embracing this style means exploring a spectrum of designs that blend classic elegance with modern flair. From flowing dresses to tailored separates, it's a celebration of individuality and self-expression.

BEAUTIFUL!

Casual Fashion Style

Casual fashion style, characterized by its relaxed yet chic vibe, prioritizes both comfort and style.

It revolves around embracing a diverse collection of versatile pieces that seamlessly blend laid-back comfort with a touch of sophistication.

At its essence, casual fashion style embodies an accessible and relaxed ethos, encouraging individuals to embrace comfort while remaining fashionable.

It allows for self-expression through easygoing and adaptable clothing choices.

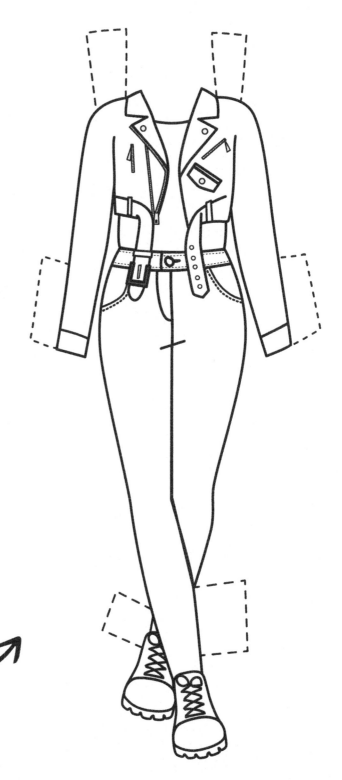

FANTASTIC!

Paper Doll Stand

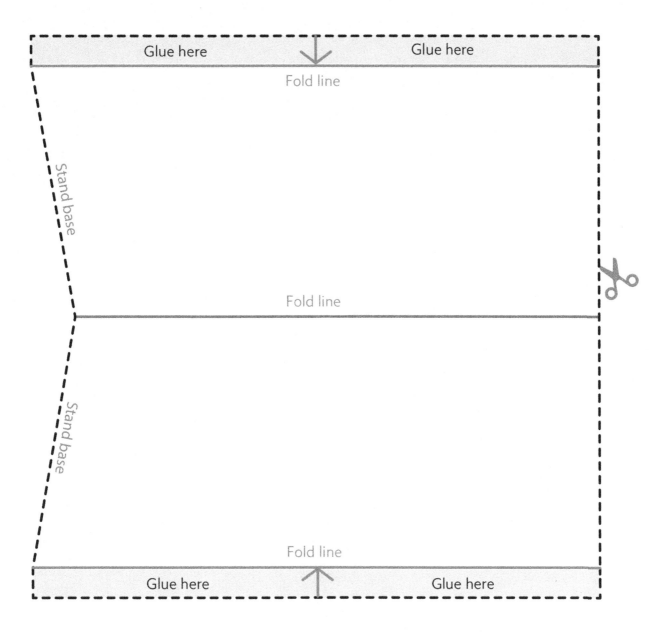

Glue here Glue here
Fold line
Stand base
Fold line
Stand base
Fold line
Glue here Glue here

Cut out the stand along the dashed lines. Then fold the stand like this:

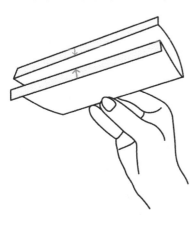

2. Glue the grey "wings" to the back side of your paper doll.

You can use tape, glue stick, or a white craft glue.

The doll will be a bit tilted backwards for better balance.

Once all done, you can start dressing the doll :)

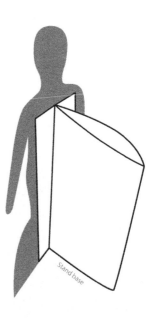

Paper Doll Stand

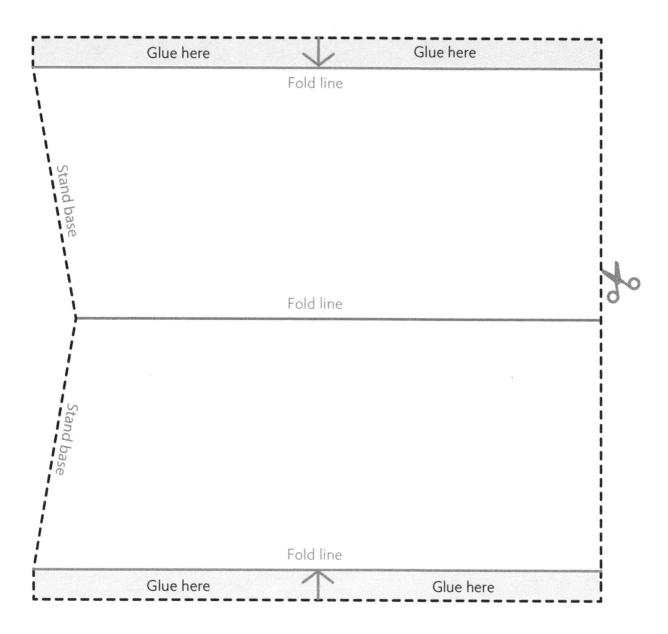

Glue here   ↓   Glue here

Fold line

Stand base

Fold line

Stand base

Fold line

Glue here   ↑   Glue here

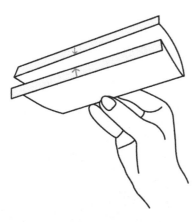

Cut out the stand along the dashed lines. Then fold the stand like this:

2. Glue the grey "wings" to the back side of your paper doll.

You can use tape, glue stick, or a white craft glue.

The doll will be a bit tilted backwards for better balance.

Once all done, you can start dressing the doll :)

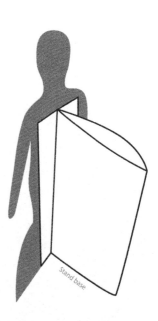

Made in the USA
Monee, IL
23 August 2024

64394753R00039